HOW TO MAKE MONEY ONLINE FROM HOME FOR YOUNG PEOPLE AND CEO

2023

HOME BASED JOB & BUSINESS IDEAS

BY

JEN SARA

Copyright © 2023 by JEN SARA

All rights reserved. No part of this publication may be reproduced, distributed, or transmitted in any form or by any means, including photocopying, recording, or other electronic or mechanical methods, without the prior written permission of the publisher, except in the case of brief quotations embodied in critical reviews and certain other noncommercial uses permitted by copyright law.

TABLE OF CONTENT

INTRODUCTION :

Julie has two small children and stayed at home with them. She loved being a mother, but she also yearned for the freedom and satisfaction that came with having a job outside the house. She was desperate to find a way to work from home and have the best of both worlds.

She stumbled across an advertisement for a program that claimed to educate individuals on how to generate money online one day while she was reading through her Facebook page. She was intrigued and clicked on the link, which took her to a website featuring testimonies from individuals who had started successful internet companies using the technique.

At first, Julie was dubious, but as she read more, the more certain she was that this was the chance she had been hoping for. After enrolling in the program, she quickly started to understand the ins and outs of generating money online.

Although the program was difficult, Julie was committed to finishing it. She devoted hours each day to her studies in website development, content creation, and online marketing. She was astounded at how much she had managed to get done so quickly.

After a short while, Julie started her online store where she sold handcrafted products. She was ecstatic to find that her goods were being purchased well and that she was making a profit. She was also happy to have more free time to spend with her kids while still feeling like she was making a financial contribution to the family.

As Julie's company grew, she was finally able to resign from her employment and operate solely from home. She was appreciative of the chance she had discovered to earn money online and pleased with the company she had established. Her children received the best of both worlds from her: a devoted stay-at-home mother and a prosperous entrepreneur.

There are several methods to earn money online from home, which have gotten more and more popular in recent years. There are possibilities to generate money online that might match your abilities and hobbies, whether you are a young person just starting out or a CEO seeking extra revenue streams.

This article will examine some of the most well-liked and profitable techniques to work from home in 2023. We'll go through the fundamentals of every strategy, provide advice for getting started, and discuss anything from online teaching and freelancing to selling goods and investing.

It's crucial to remember that earning money online is not a get-rich-quick program and that success will involve hard work and perseverance. The optimal strategy will rely on your particular circumstances and objectives since each technique has its own set of advantages and disadvantages. You will have a better grasp of the numerous online income streams at the conclusion of this course and be able to choose the one that suits you the most.

OVERVIEW OF WAYS TO MAKE MONEY ONLINE FROM HOME IN 2023

There are several options to work from home and earn money online in 2023, including:

When a consumer puts in an order, the firm purchases the requested item from a third-party supplier, who then sends it straight to the customer. This business model is known as drop shipping.

Online one-on-one or group instruction for students is referred to as online tutoring or online teaching.

Offering your expertise and services to customers on a project- or contract basis is known as freelancing.

Online surveys: taking part in market research studies by responding to survey questions.

Purchasing and selling assets in the expectation that their value would rise over time is known as investing in stocks and cryptocurrencies.

Selling goods or services via an online shop or platform like Amazon, Etsy, or eBay is known as e-commerce or using online marketplaces.

Creation and monetization of content: Producing and making money from material on websites like YouTube, TikTok, or Twitch.

Online coaching or consulting: Giving customers suggestions, direction, or services online.

Earn money by advertising the goods and services of other people via affiliate marketing.

Microtasks or online data entry: doing quick, easy tasks for pennies on the dollar.

It's vital to remember that, before beginning an internet business, it's crucial to do extensive research, comprehend the target audience, market, competition, and the venture's legal and financial ramifications, as well as exercise caution and be aware of any frauds. In addition, it's crucial to have a clear plan, be patient, and be open to changing market conditions.

CHAPTER 1

E-COMMERCE AND ONLINE MARKETPLACES

Selling goods or services through an online shop platform is a common method to generate money online. This is known as e-commerce. Without having to create and manage their own websites, individuals and small companies may sell their goods to a big audience on online marketplaces like Amazon, Etsy, and eBay.

Typically, in order to begin selling in an online marketplace, you must:

1. Register for an account: Create an account on the marketplace and fill out the required fields, including your company name and contact information.

2. List your stuff here: Make listings for the items you wish to sell and provide thorough details such as the title, description, pricing, and photographs.

3. Fulfill orders: After a consumer puts a purchase, you must manage the shipping and packing details to deliver the goods to the customer.

4. Provide customer service: Address questions from clients and resolve any problems that may develop.

Using online marketplaces may be a terrific method to test the market for your goods and a low-cost option to reach a wide audience. But it also needs a solid grasp of marketing and e-commerce, as well as the capacity to manage logistics and customer care.

CONSIDERATIONS AND CAUTION WHEN BEGINNING AN ONLINE VENTURE

When beginning an internet business, it's crucial to do your homework and exercise caution. You may better grasp the market, the target market, the competitors, and the venture's financial and legal ramifications by doing research. It may also assist you in defining a clear plan and identifying possible dangers and possibilities.

Researching can assist you with:
1. Recognize the market: Researching the market will help you get a sense of its size, pace of expansion, and trends.
2. Determine your target market. Knowing your market can help you develop a product or service that will appeal to their requirements and preferences.
3. Examine the competition. By understanding what other businesses are doing, you can spot possibilities and steer clear of problems.
4. Recognize the legal and financial ramifications: Investigating the legal and financial ramifications of your organization may help you comprehend the rules and specifications that apply to it, as well as the prospective expenses and income streams.
When beginning an internet business, caution is also essential. It's crucial to be cautious when exchanging

personal or financial information online and to be aware of possible scams and fraudulent schemes. Be prepared to tackle the dangers and difficulties that come with beginning an internet business by being aware of them.

It's crucial to remember that beginning an internet business is not a guarantee of success; it requires perseverance, hard effort, and devotion. It's critical to have reasonable expectations and to be prepared to change course when required.

ONLINE MARKETS AND E-COMMERCE:

Selling goods or services through an online shop or platform is a common method to generate money online. This is known as e-commerce. Without having to create and manage their own websites, individuals and small companies may sell their goods to a big audience on online marketplaces like Amazon, Etsy, and eBay.

You may access a wide audience and take use of the marketplace's established infrastructure, such as payment processing and customer care, by leveraging online marketplaces. Online marketplaces may also provide useful information on consumer behavior and preferences, which can assist guide your product development and marketing initiatives.

However, it's crucial to remember that there is stiff competition in online marketplaces, making it crucial to carry out careful research and create a compelling marketing plan in order to stand out. It's crucial to take into account the fact that online marketplaces charge fees for accessing their platform when developing your pricing strategy and business plan.

Overall, online marketplaces and e-commerce may be fantastic ways to earn money, but it's crucial to do your homework, have a clear plan, and be ready to adjust as the market does.

CREATING AN ONLINE STORE AND TRANSACTING IN GOODS or SERVICES THERE

It's common to set up an online shop to offer goods or services in order to generate money online. The general procedures for setting up an internet shop are as follows:

1. Select a market segment or product line: Decide if you want to market a service, a product that can be purchased online, or both.
2. Select an e-commerce platform: You may develop and host your online shop using a variety of e-commerce platforms, including Shopify, BigCommerce, and Wix.
3. Register a domain name: Pick a domain name for your online shop, which will serve as the URL that users will type into their browsers to access it.
4. Design and modify your store: Make your store's layout and design pleasing to the eye and user-friendly.
5. Creating your own items, purchasing them in bulk from a supplier, or using a dropshipping service are all options for where to get your products from.
6. Set up payment and shipment: Establish payment procedures so that consumers can buy things and delivery choices so that customers may get their orders.

7. Promote your business, which may be done via advertising, social media marketing, content marketing, and SEO (SEO).

Order fulfillment and customer service management: You will be in charge of managing the logistics of delivering things to clients and resolving any potential problems with customer care.

It's crucial to remember that creating an internet business is not an easy process and it takes time.

UTILIZING PLATFORMS LIKE AMAZON OR ETSY TO REACH A WIDER AUDIENCE

It's common for people and small companies to use websites like Amazon or Etsy to attract a larger audience in order to monetize their internet presence. These platforms provide you access to a ready-made consumer base and may greatly improve the exposure of your goods or services. The following are the main procedures for utilizing online marketplaces like Amazon or Etsy to offer goods or services:

Open a new account: Create an account on the marketplace by filling out the required information, including your company name and contact information.

Add your items here: Make listings for the items you wish to sell and provide thorough details such as the title, description, pricing, and photographs.

Order fulfillment is managing the logistics of delivering the goods to the consumer, including packing and shipping, when a customer placed an order.

Respond to client questions and deal with any problems that may occur while providing customer care.

You may access a wider audience and take use of the marketplace's established infrastructure, such as payment processing and customer care, by leveraging platforms like Amazon or Etsy. These platforms may also provide you with useful information about consumer behavior and preferences, which you can use to guide your marketing and product development efforts. On these platforms, there are a lot of rivalries, so it's crucial to do your homework thoroughly and come up with a solid marketing plan if you want to stand out. It's crucial to take into account the fact that these platforms also charge a fee for accessing them when developing your pricing strategy and business plan.

CHAPTER 2 :

BLOGGING AND YOUTUBE

The process of regularly generating and posting information online, often in the form of blog posts on a personal website or another platform, is known as blogging. A broad variety of subjects, including lifestyle, personal experiences, news, reviews, opinion, and more, may be covered via blogging, which can be done for either personal or professional reasons. A personal website or a blogging platform like WordPress, Tumblr, or Blogger are all options for blogging.

On the other hand, YouTube provides a platform for sharing and viewing videos that users may post. A Google subsidiary, YouTube is a popular platform for making and sharing videos. It lets users create their own channels, submit films, and monetize their material via adverts, sponsorships, and other methods. YouTube is one of the most widely used platforms for making and sharing videos, and it may be used for entertainment, education, and personal or professional reasons.

Making and distributing material on a particular subject or niche via blogging and YouTube video creation are two well-liked methods to generate money online.

The basic steps to launch a blog or YouTube channel are as follows:

1. Select a subject or niche: Make a decision on a particular topic or niche that you are enthusiastic about and that you think you can consistently produce material for.

2. Create a website or YouTube channel: You may share your material on a website you create or a YouTube channel you create.

3. Produce worthwhile material: Consistently produce and distribute high-quality information that is relevant to your specialty or area of interest.

4 . Build an audience by promoting your content and interacting with it via email marketing, social media, and other channels.

5. Earn money from your blog or YouTube channel through a variety of methods, including product sales, affiliate marketing, sponsored articles, and advertising.

The ability to succeed in internet businesses like blogging and YouTube requires a lot of time, effort, and commitment. It's crucial to have a clear plan, to be patient, and to be open to change as the market does. Before beginning, it's also crucial to comprehend the possible legal and financial repercussions of producing money via YouTube and blogging.

GENERATING A FOLLOWER AND GENERATING PROFITS THROUGH ADVERTISING, AFFILIATE MARKETING, OR SPONSORED CONTENT

Building a following is the process of growing and interacting with a blog or YouTube channel audience. This entails producing worthwhile content, disseminating it through numerous platforms, and interacting with the audience via social media, comments, and other channels. Increasing exposure and drawing in an audience who is interested in the information being produced are the two main objectives of following-building.

The technique of making money from a blog or YouTube channel is known as monetizing. A blog or YouTube channel may be made profitable in a number of ways, including via advertising, affiliate marketing, and sponsored material.

Advertising is putting up adverts on a blog or YouTube channel and being paid depending on how many people click on or watch them.

Affiliate marketing is a performance-based marketing method in which a company pays one or more affiliates for each visitor or client that affiliates generate on their own via marketing.

Content that has been sponsored is material that has been paid for by a brand. The material is produced at the brand's expense and posted on the blog or YouTube channel to advertise its goods and services.

In conclusion, cultivating and engaging an audience is the process of establishing a following, and monetizing is the process of making money from that audience via different channels like advertising, affiliate marketing, or sponsored content.

SUGGESTIONS FOR GENERATING ENGAGING, HIGH-QUALITY CONTENT

The process of developing and disseminating worthwhile and engaging material on a blog or YouTube channel that will draw in and keep an audience is referred to as creating high-quality, engaging content. It's a strategy for producing educational, amusing, and practical material that will keep viewers engaged in the blog or YouTube channel, improving the likelihood of audience growth and revenue generation for the blog or channel.

Tips for producing high-quality, engaging content are recommendations or pieces of advice on how to raise the caliber and level of participation in the material being created. These pointers can include knowing your target market, producing material consistently, being genuine, leveraging images, optimizing for search engines, fostering interaction, disseminating information, advertising the content, and paying attention to audience comments.

Here are some pointers for producing top-notch, compelling content:

1. Know your audience: Recognize your target market's identity and the needs of your market. Make sure your material is relevant to their wants and requirements.
2. Be consistent: Consistently produce and regularly distribute fresh material. This keeps your viewers interested and returning for more.
3. Be genuine. Stay loyal to your business and yourself. Authenticity will increase your audience's trust in you and make your material more relevant.
4. Use photos, videos, and infographics to enhance the visual appeal and readability of your information.
5. Optimize for search engines: To make it simpler for people to locate your material via search engines, include keywords in your content and optimize your titles, descriptions, and tags.
6. Encourage audience interaction with your material by posing questions, conducting polls, or including interactive features.
7. Share your knowledge and skills on the subject you are blogging or vlogging about. By doing so, you can position yourself as an expert in the industry and provide your audience with something of value.
8. Promote your content through social media, email marketing, and other techniques to expand the audience for it.
9. Pay attention to audience input. Take note of audience feedback and use it in your content and strategy as a whole.

It takes time and works to produce high-quality, interesting material, but by implementing these suggestions, you may improve your chances of gaining subscribers and making money from your blog or YouTube channel.

CHAPTER 3:

FREELANCE SERVICES

Instead of working for a business or organization, freelance services refer to the work done by independent contractors.

Freelancers provide a variety of services, such as but not limited to the:

Writing: Independent writers provide written material for a range of media, including websites, blogs, magazines, newspapers, and books. They have the ability to write about a wide range of subjects, including news, culture, technology, and more.

Graphic Design: Using text, space, image, and color, graphic design is the process of visually communicating and solving problems. To produce visual material like as logos, brochures, website layouts, and social media graphics, graphic designers employ a variety of applications and tools.

There are many different kinds of marketing products that may incorporate graphic design, like:

Resources for Branding (Logos, Business Cards, Letterheads)

Promotional Materials (Brochures, Flyers, Posters)

Promotional Materials (Billboards, Magazine Ads, Online Ads)

Package Layout (Product Packaging, Label Design)

Web Page Layout (Layout, Icons, Graphics)

Graphic designers use a wide range of methods and aesthetics to produce visually attractive designs,

Including:

Using diverse fonts and typesetting to provide visual hierarchy and emphasis is known as typography.

Understanding how colors may arouse feelings and generate contrast is known as color theory.

Composing entails placing items on a page in a way that promotes movement and balance.

The art of making straightforward, identifiable symbols or visuals.

Designing motion graphics, packaging, logos, or user interfaces and user experiences are some of the specialties available to graphic designers.

They may work in-house for a Business, for an Agency, or as Independent Contractors.

Graphic designers need to be imaginative and have a keen sense of beauty, but they also need to be technically proficient and knowledgeable about design tools like Adobe Illustrator, Photoshop, and InDesign. In order to develop designs that are not only aesthetically beautiful but also successful in accomplishing their intended aim, graphic designers need also have a solid grasp of branding, marketing, and user experience concepts.

CODING :

Independent The act of writing instructions that a computer can comprehend and carry out is known as programming, commonly referred to as coding. Programmers develop code that may be used to construct software applications, websites, and other kinds of computer programs using programming languages including Python, Java, C++, and JavaScript.

Programming comes in a wide variety, including:

Web development is the process of building websites and web-based programs utilizing coding languages like HTML, CSS, and JavaScript.

building applications for mobile devices utilizing programming languages like Swift for iOS and Kotlin for Android.

Video games are developed utilizing programming languages like C++ and C#.

Data science and machine learning include analyzing data and developing machine learning models using programming languages like Python and R.

Writing code that communicates with an operating system, such as kernels and drivers, is known as systems programming.

A programmer may choose from a wide range of job choices since programming is a talent in high demand. Programmers may work as freelancers or in-house employees for businesses, and they can pursue a variety of specializations, including web development, mobile app development, game development, and data science.

Strong logical and problem-solving abilities, as well as the capacity for abstract thought and experience with complicated systems, are necessary for programming. Programmers should be knowledgeable about various programming languages and tools as well as current with emerging technology and business trends. Additionally, as they often work in teams and must be able to communicate their code and concepts to non-technical coworkers, programmers should be strong communicators.

Freelance Social Media Management The process of developing, publishing, and maintaining material on social media sites like Facebook, Instagram, Twitter, and LinkedIn is referred to as social media management. Social media managers work with companies and people to manage their social media accounts, generate content, interact with followers, and execute social media plans.

Various duties are included in social media management, such as:

Creating a content calendar and scheduling posts beforehand

Writing subtitles, choosing photos and videos, and producing compelling material

Utilizing technologies to measure engagement, reach, and follower development when measuring and assessing performance

Responding to comments and messages, building and managing groups and communities, and engaging with followers

Working with the marketing, advertising, and customer support teams is an example of collaborating with other teams.

keeping up on best practices, trends, and new features

The administration of social media might be done in-house or by a freelancer. A social media manager has to be knowledgeable about the various platforms, their capabilities, and the best practices for content creation and publication. They should also be good writers and communicators with the capacity to communicate and engage with audiences. In order to provide material that is in line with the client's aims and goals, the social media manager should also have a solid awareness of the client's target audience, branding, and marketing concepts.

PHOTOGRAPHER :

Independent The skill of using a camera to capture pictures is called photography. A photographer may capture images of everything and anything, and they can choose to focus on several types of photography, including street, product, event, and portrait photography.

Typically, professional photographers will have a wide range of tools at their disposal, including cameras, lenses, lighting, and other accessories. Additionally, they will be well-versed in composition, lighting, and post-processing strategies.

Here are a few popular categories of photography:

Portrait photography is the art of taking pictures of individuals, either in a studio or outside.

Product photography is the practice of taking pictures of goods for use in advertising or online sales.

Photographing occasions like weddings, parties, and concerts are known as event photography.

Photographing natural landscapes, urban vistas, and other outside settings are known as landscape photography.

Street photography is the art of taking unposed pictures of people and environments in public places.

You may work as a photographer full-time, as a freelancer, or just for fun. In addition to having a keen aesthetic eye and originality, a professional photographer will have a solid grasp of the technical components of photography, such as lighting, composition, and post-processing. They should also be able to communicate well and do business since they often engage with customers and must be able to justify their prices.

VIRTUAL ASSISTANCE :

Freelance virtual assistance Remotely assisting customers with their personal and administrative needs is known as virtual assistance (VA). Virtual assistants (VAs) often engage with customers through email, instant messaging, and video conferencing while working remotely or from a home office.

Among the duties, a VA may assist with are the following:

Responding to and arranging emails under email management

managing the calendar, scheduling meetings, and appointments

inserting information into databases or spreadsheets
Managing and publishing on social media accounts is known as social media management.
Research: carrying out an internet search
Making travel arrangements: Travel planning
Customer service: responding to questions and complaints from customers
The provision of virtual support might be a full-time endeavor, a freelance one, or a side business. An effective virtual assistant should be detail-oriented, organized, and able to multitask.
They should also be effective communicators since they often interact with customers and must be able to articulate their concepts and charges.
The technology and resources required for their jobs, such as email, instant messaging, and video conferencing applications, as well as office programs like Microsoft Office and Google Suite, should also be known to VAs.

TRANSCRIPT :
Independent Transcribing audio or video data into text is the process of transcription. As they listen to audio files, transcriptionists put what they hear into a written document.
Transcription is possible in a variety of domains,

Including:
Transcribing court hearings, depositions, and other legal documents are known as legal transcription.
Transcribing medical records, patient histories, and other medical papers is known as medical transcription.
Interview transcription, podcast transcription, and other forms of entertainment-related audio transcription.
Meeting transcription, conference call transcription, and other business-related audio transcription.

One may work as a transcriptionist full-time, as a freelancer, or as a side business.

In addition to having a fast typing speed, transcriptionists should also have strong listening and attention to detail-abilities.

They should also be knowledgeable about the jargon used in their particular sector of transcribing, such as any legal or medical phrases. They should also be conversant with office programs like Microsoft Office as well as tools and software for transcribing.

Interpretation:

Independent The process of transferring written material from one language to another is called translation. When creating a new version of a written text in a foreign language, translators work to maintain the meaning, style, and tone of the original text as closely as they can.

There are several disciplines in which translation is possible, including:

Translating technical materials and instructions in disciplines like engineering, medicine, and technology is known as technical translation.

Legal translation involves the translation of legal documents such as contracts, statutes, and patents.

Translating novels, poems, and other literary works are known as literary translation.

Translation of websites and online material for international audiences.

One may work as a translator full-time, as a freelancer, or as a side business. The content, style, and tone of the original material should be accurately translated by translators who are fluent in both the source language and the target language. They should also be conversant with the jargon used in their particular area of translation, such as any technical or legal phrases. They should also be proficient writers who are knowledgeable with translation tools and software.

Freelancers might work on a project basis, part-time, or full-time, and they can specialize in one or more services. Flexibility, independence, and the freedom to choose the customers and projects one wants to work on are all benefits of freelancing.

The basic stages of beginning a freelancing company are as follows:

1. Describe Your Services And Skills:

The process of locating, evaluating, and expressing a person's talents and abilities is referred to as "identifying one's skills and services." It is a crucial phase in career development and job hunting because it enables people to recognize their advantages and disadvantages and articulate them clearly to prospective employers or customers.

People should think about their education, training, job experience, and personal interests when selecting talents and services. They need to reflect on the duties and obligations they have previously carried out, as well as the knowledge and skills necessary to finish them.

Examples of abilities and offerings that a person could mention include:

Ability to write well-crafted papers and reports thanks to strong writing abilities

strong analytical abilities, with the ability to evaluate facts and provide insights.

Effectively interact with a variety of stakeholders thanks to strong communication skills.

Strong project management abilities; capable of organizing, planning, and supervising projects.

strong technical abilities; adept at using a variety of programs and tools.

Strong customer service abilities; able to provide consumers with exceptional service.

It's crucial to remember that services and talents may take many different forms; they are not only restricted to professional capabilities but can include non-professional skills that might be valuable in the workplace.

2. Make A Portfolio:

A portfolio is a collection of work samples, accomplishment proof, and other pertinent data that displays a person's knowledge, skills, and experience. Professionals like authors, designers, and painters often utilize it to present their work to prospective customers, jobs, or educational institutions.

A portfolio may also include images, videos, and other digital files that highlight a person's abilities and accomplishments when it comes to online employment. It acts as a tool for showcasing a person's skills, credentials, and experiences to prospective clients, customers, or employers.

A physical book or binder, a website, or a digital presentation may all be used to build a portfolio. A portfolio may be customized for a particular field or position, and it should be frequently updated with fresh, relevant work examples. Making ensuring the portfolio is well-structured, simple to use, and showcases the person's greatest work and accomplishments are crucial.

3. Create a Professional Profile:

Creating and maintaining an online presence that highlights a person's abilities, credentials, and experience is referred to as building a professional profile. A person may use it to network with other experts in their industry and to sell themselves to possible employers, clients, or consumers.

Typically, a professional profile has the following details:

Education And Qualifications: information about degrees, diplomas, and other educational achievements

Work Experience: Previous Employment, Internships, and Other Experience

Skills: Knowledge and abilities in a person's sector or business, both professional and personal.

Projects: any tasks or examples of work that the person has performed and wishes to display

Awards and achievements: whatever honors or accolades the person has gotten

Contact Information: The person's contact details, including their email address, phone number, and social network accounts

It is possible to construct professional profiles on a variety of websites, including LinkedIn, Indeed, and Glassdoor. In order to exhibit the most current and relevant information, it is crucial to maintain these accounts periodically updated with fresh information, abilities, and work examples.

It's also crucial to keep in mind that a professional profile encompasses more than just an individual's online persona; it also takes into account how they portray themselves in person, including how they dress, how they interact with others, and how they behave in formal situations.

4. Network :

To find out about new prospects and market your skills, connect with other freelancers and experts in your industry.

A network is, in broad words, a collection of entities that are linked together and may interact and share resources.

A network, in the context of computer technology, is a collection of linked computers and other gadgets, such as servers, routers, and switches, that may exchange information and share resources.

The practice of establishing and sustaining connections with other professionals in the same or a related industry is referred to as networking in the context of business and professional growth. It may include things like going to networking events, joining groups for professionals, and interacting with other professionals on social media. The goal of networking is to create contacts and connections that may result in business possibilities, such as job offers, clients, or joint ventures.

Networks are the pattern of connections between a collection of people, organizations, or other entities. It is possible to study these linkages, which might be social, economic, or professional in character, to learn how information, resources, and power move throughout the group.

A set of interconnected radio stations, television stations, or other communication channels that are joined together to exchange content, resources, or other information is referred to as a network in the communications industry.

5. Attract Clients :

The process of collecting and keeping consumers or clients for a company or a person is referred to as "getting clients." It might encompass tasks like marketing, advertising, and networking and is crucial to operating a successful company.

Examples of strategies for attracting customers include:

Building and maintaining connections with other professionals in the same or a similar industry via networking might result in new business opportunities or employment offers.

Marketing is the use of a variety of strategies, including public relations, advertising, and content marketing, to sell a product or service and draw in customers.

Cold calling is the practice of personally contacting prospective customers via phone or email to present yourself and your services.

Asking current customers to recommend your services to their friends, family, and coworkers is known as a referral.

Online presence: Establishing and maintaining a presence online using a website, social media channels, and a professional profile to attract customers and highlight your skills.

It's crucial to understand that obtaining customers is a continuous process rather than an isolated occurrence. Keeping a regular stream of customers, takes tenacity, inventiveness, and consistent work. To provide a great service that fits their wants, it's also critical to comprehend the needs and expectations of your consumers and personalize your services appropriately.

6 . Set Your Rates :

Setting your prices is the process of figuring out how much the services you provide as a person or a company will cost. It is a crucial element in operating a successful company since it enables you to define your worth and draw in the ideal customers.

You should take into account a number of elements, such as:

the price of your time, including the time you spend working on the job, as well as any supplementary expenses like supplies or tools.

The price you paid for your knowledge, which includes your training, education, and experience.
the price of your rivals, including the charges made by other companies or people working in your industry.
Your target market's cost, as well as prospective customers' spending plans and expectations.
There are several techniques for determining your rates, including:
Hourly rate: charging, for instance, $50 per hour for your services.
Charging a fixed fee for a particular project, such as $500 for website design, is known as a project rate.
Value-based pricing: Calculating fees based on the benefits your services provide to customers.
It's crucial to remember that your charges should accurately represent the value of your services and that they should take into account not just the expense of your time and expertise but also the value that your customers will get from your services. In order to have a strong working connection with your customers, it's also crucial to be flexible with your pricing and open to negotiations, particularly when you're just starting out.

7. Handle Your Money:
Organizing, planning, and efficiently administering the financial resources of a company or a person is referred to as managing your money. It entails tasks including setting up and following a budget, maintaining correct financial records and making wise financial judgments.
Several examples of effective money management strategies include:
Making a strategy for your financial allocation and spending, then adhering to it can help you stay within your means.

To get a comprehensive view of your financial condition, maintain detailed records of all financial activities, including income and spending.

To guarantee that you get paid on time, you must swiftly and effectively create and deliver invoices to customers.

Financial planning is the process of coming up with a strategy for achieving long-term financial objectives, such as paying off debt or saving for retirement.

Investment: Making informed financial decisions in order to build your wealth over time.

Tax planning is the process of staying current with tax rules and regulations in order to reduce your tax burden.

It's crucial to keep in mind that handling your money is a continuous activity, not a one-time thing.

To ensure that you are on the proper path to attaining your financial objectives, it is necessary to continuously monitor, analyze, and adapt to your situation. Additionally, it's crucial to get expert guidance when necessary.

An accountant or financial adviser may assist you in developing a financial strategy that benefits both you and your company.

8. Constantly Enhance:

The phrase "Continually Improve" describes the continuing process of detecting, assessing, and making adjustments to increase the effectiveness and performance of a company, a procedure, or a system. It is a way of thinking and doing that places more emphasis on gradual, small-scale improvements than on abrupt, massive transformations.

The following are some instances of techniques to constantly improve:

Identifying opportunities for improvement entails regularly evaluating how a company, process, or system is operating and identifying areas where improvements may be made to increase effectiveness or efficiency.

Data analysis is the process of gathering and examining statistics, such as financial data, performance indicators, or customer feedback, to identify areas that need improvement.

Implementing adjustments: Rather than attempting to implement significant changes all at once, make tiny, gradual improvements to increase performance.

Monitoring and evaluating development throughout time to make sure that adjustments are having the intended impact and that advancements are being made.

Encourage workers to actively participate in the process of improvement and to express their thoughts and opinions through promoting employee engagement.

Continuous learning involves following industry trends and best practices as well as constantly picking up new skills from others.

A crucial component of every business is a continuous improvement since it enables a corporation to adjust and develop in response to changes in the market, the economy, and technology. It contributes to the development of an innovative, efficient, and customer-focused culture that may boost output, profitability, and client happiness.

Although it might be a terrific method to earn money online, freelancing also demands effort and commitment. It is crucial to have a clear plan, to be patient, and to be open to change as the market does. Before beginning, it's also critical to comprehend any possible legal and financial repercussions of freelancing.

BUILDING A PORTFOLIO AND FINDING CLIENTS ON PLATFORMS LIKE UPWORK OR FIVERR AND OFFERING SKILLS LIKE WRITING, GRAPHIC DESIGN, OR PROGRAMMING

It's common for freelancers to use websites like Upwork or Fiverr to advertise their writing, graphic design, or programming abilities in order to find customers and earn money online.

These platforms provide independent contractors with an easy method to present their abilities and expertise to customers searching for certain services. The following are the standard procedures for listing talents on websites like Upwork or Fiverr:

Open a new account: Create an account on the site by filling out the required fields about your qualifications, work history, and portfolio.

Making a portfolio Make a portfolio that highlights your abilities and background. Examples of your work, client endorsements, and other relevant certificates or qualifications might be included.

Find customers: Look through the platform's job postings and submit an application for positions that fit your background and experience. You may also get in touch with prospective customers personally and introduce yourself.

Choose your prices: Set your charges in accordance with your qualifications and expertise, and be ready to haggle with customers.

Communicate with customers: Keep in touch with your clients as the project progresses to make sure they are pleased with your work and to handle any potential problems.

Receive payment: The customer will pay you via the platform after the job is finished.

Freelancers may access a variety of customers and projects by listing their abilities on websites like Upwork or Fiverr, and they can make use of the infrastructure already in place on such websites, such as payment processing and dispute resolution.

But you must remember that there is fierce competition on these platforms, so you must have a good portfolio and sell your services skillfully.

It's crucial to include this in your pricing plan since these platforms also impose costs for accessing their system.

CHAPTER3 :

ONLINE TRADING

Online trading is the practice of purchasing and selling financial assets using an electronic platform, such as a website or mobile app, as opposed to a conventional brick-and-mortar brokerage. Investors may trade a variety of financial products, including stocks, bonds, options, futures, and other assets, using online trading platforms.

Trades can be executed more quickly and effectively since there is less need for human interaction throughout the process.

Online trading platforms also provide users immediate access to market data, analytical tools, and other sources of information that may help traders make well-informed choices.

With the introduction of internet trading, small investors now have more options to engage in the financial markets, increasing their prospects to increase their wealth.

However, it's crucial to keep in mind that there are risks associated with online trading, so before making an investment, it's vital to familiarize yourself with the market and comprehend the dangers.

Online trading platforms include, for instance:

Online stockbrokers include companies like E*TRADE and TD Ameritrade that provide online marketplaces for buying and selling equities.

Online forex trading platforms, including Plus500 and Metatrader, are ones that let users trade in foreign currencies.

Online options trading systems, like OptionsXpress and TradeStation, are those that let users trade options contracts.

Online trading may be advantageous for a variety of factors, including:

CONVENIENCE :

Convenience is the quality of being simple to use, obtain, or comprehend. It is often used to describe things that are easy, quick, and straightforward to handle.

Convenience is one of the main advantages that online trading platforms provide in terms of trading online. Investors may use a computer or mobile device with internet connectivity to purchase and sell stocks anytime, anywhere. The online platforms provide quicker transaction execution, real-time access to market data, and a plethora of information and research tools. They are accessible around the clock. Small investors now find it easier to join the financial markets, creating more opportunities for them to increase their wealth.

There are several additional areas of life where convenience may be used, such as:

A convenient location is one that is accessible to the general public and is simple to reach.

A rapid and simple payment mechanism is referred to as being convenient.

Customer service that is convenient is readily available and offers prompt beneficial support.

Technology that makes our life simpler and more productive is referred to as convenient technology.

CHEAPER PRICE :

Reduced expenditures or the amount of money required to create an item or service are referred to as lower costs. The reverse of rising expenses is this.

Lower expenses in the context of online trading relate to the fees and charges that these platforms often impose that are lower than those imposed by conventional brick-and-mortar brokerage companies. Since of these decreased expenses, traders are able to retain a larger portion of their earnings because they don't have to pay the broker as many fees and commissions. For small investors who do not have as many funds to invest, this can be very helpful.

Reduced expenses are also applicable in other situations, such as:

Lower production costs: the decrease in costs associated with manufacturing a something or service, which may aid a business in boosting earnings.

Lower operational costs: the decrease in company expenditures such as rent, utilities, and wages.

Lower prices: a product or service's price decreases, which may increase its accessibility and affordability for customers.

It's crucial to remember that cheaper prices don't necessarily equate to inferior quality. Businesses may save expenses while still offering high-quality products and services.

SPEED :

The pace at which something moves works, or happens is referred to as its speed. Speed in online trading refers to the capacity to receive market data and make judgments in real time, as well as the capacity to carry out deals rapidly and efficiently. This may provide traders a benefit in quick-moving markets where every second matters and enable them to seize trading opportunities as they present themselves.

Speed may also be used in many situations, such as:

Movement speed is the pace at which a person or an item moves.

The pace at which information is conveyed is referred to as communication speed.

The pace at which a computer or other device can process data is known as the speed of processing.

The pace at which a service is delivered is known as the speed of delivery.

Delivery speed is the pace at which a product is delivered.

It's crucial to remember that speed may be a double-edged sword; although it might be advantageous to execute transactions rapidly in fast-moving markets if managed improperly, it can also result in rash judgments and blunders. It's crucial to strike a balance between prudence and speed.

Numerous kinds of securities and financial products are accessible for trading on an internet trading platform, which is referred to as having a large variety of financial instruments. This may apply to assets such as stocks, bonds, options, futures, and more. Being able to participate in a number of markets and industries and diversify their portfolios thanks to the availability of a broad range of financial instruments may help traders reduce risk and improve their chances of success.

Various types of financial instruments that may be traded include:

Stocks may be purchased or sold on a stock market and represent a portion of ownership in a publicly listed corporation.

Bonds: a loan to a business or government that comes with a set rate of interest.

Options: provide the owner the choice—but not the obligation—to purchase or dispose of the underlying asset at a certain price on or before a predetermined date.

Futures are agreements that require either the buyer or the seller to acquire or sell a certain asset at a specified price and date in the future.

Forex: Foreign exchange trade, where a variety of currencies may be bought and sold.

The capacity to swiftly respond to market changes and greater possibilities to benefit from market movements may both be facilitated by having a large variety of financial instruments at the disposal of traders. It's crucial to remember that possessing a broad variety of financial instruments does not ensure success. Before making an investment, traders should undertake extensive study and understand the risks and possible benefits of each instrument.

The capacity to get or receive information that is required or requested is referred to as having access to information. The capacity to access market data, research resources and other information that may assist traders in making knowledgeable judgments is referred to as access to information in the context of online trading.

A multitude of data and research tools are available on online trading platforms, including real-time market data, technical analysis, news updates, and other market research. By doing so, traders may better understand market conditions, and spot patterns, and execute transactions. Additionally, a lot of online trading platforms provide instructional materials that may assist traders to improve their knowledge and abilities, such as webinars, tutorials, and other tools.

Additionally, access to information may be used in various situations, such as:

Healthcare access refers to the availability of necessary medical treatment.

The capacity to pursue education is known as access to education.

The capacity to get legal counsel and representation are known as access to legal services.

Technology usage is referred to as having access to technology.

It's vital to remember that having access to information does not ensure success, therefore it's crucial to utilize it intelligently and to take the source and trustworthiness of the material into consideration.

AUTOMATION :

Automation is the use of technology to complete a job or process without the involvement of a person. Automation in the context of online trading refers to the use of computer programs and algorithms that can carry out deals and control risk on the trader's behalf.

Stop-loss orders, automated trading techniques, and other tools are available on online trading platforms, which may assist traders in managing risk and placing better-educated transactions. A stop-loss order, for instance, is a request made to a broker to sell an asset when its price reaches a certain level; this might assist to minimize losses in the event that the market swings against the deal. Automated trading strategies are pre-programmed rules or directives that carry out transactions in accordance with certain criteria, such as moving averages or other technical indicators.

Additionally, automation may be used in various situations, such as:

Automation in manufacturing refers to the use of tools and technology to carry out operations that were once handled by people.

Automation in transportation refers to the use of technology, such as self-driving automobiles, to manage and observe moving objects.

Using chatbots and other technology to respond to customer support requests and inquiries is known as automation in customer service.

It's crucial to remember that although automation may increase speed and efficiency, it also carries a number of dangers and restrictions, including the possibility of mistakes, a lack of flexibility, and a lack of human supervision.

CUSTOMIZATION :

Customization is the act of altering or changing anything in order to satisfy the unique requirements or preferences of a person or group. Customization in the context of online trading refers to the capability to adjust the trading platform to the preferences of the specific trader, such as by adding indicators, alerts, and other tools.

Many online trading platforms let users add indicators, alerts, and other tools to make the platform more suited to their tastes and trading style. This may include technical indicators to assist in spot market trends and patterns, such as moving averages or the relative strength index. The ability to establish alerts, such as price alerts that may warn the trader when a certain price is achieved, is another feature that many platforms provide to traders.

Other situations in which customization is appropriate to include:

Customization of goods refers to the capacity to alter a good to satisfy the unique requirements of a client.

The capacity to adapt a service to a customer's unique demands is known as service customization.

Website customization refers to the capacity to alter the structure, operation, and appearance of a website to suit the preferences of the user.

It's crucial to remember that although customization might be advantageous in terms of efficiency and personalization, it can also have its own set of dangers and restrictions, including the possibility of mistakes, a lack of flexibility, and a lack of supervision. It's crucial to use care and, if necessary, seek expert guidance.

RISK:

Risk is the chance of losing anything valuable, like cash, property, or life. It may also allude to the potential for anything bad to occur, like harm or failure.

Risk in the context of online trading refers to the potential for financial loss brought on by changes in the market or subpar investing choices. For instance, there is a chance of losing money while investing in the stock market due to shifts in the market or business performance. Online trading is also subject to additional dangers including fraud, hackers, and technological difficulties.

The risk may also be used in various situations, including:

Risk in business is the potential for financial loss brought on by subpar management or unfavorable market circumstances.

Risk in finance is the potential for financial loss brought on by subpar investment choices or market circumstances.

Risk in insurance is the chance that a loss will occur that is covered by a policy.

Risk in healthcare is the chance that surgery or therapy will have a detrimental impact on one's health.

It's crucial to keep in mind that risk is a necessary component of every investment or company endeavor and that managing risk is essential for making wise choices.

This may include doing due diligence on prospective investments, diversifying portfolios, and using risk management techniques.

Investing in securities, cryptocurrencies, or other online trading platforms

Using money to buy financial assets with the hope of getting a return on investment is the process of investing in stocks, cryptocurrencies, or other types of online trading. It is a technique for people or organizations to gradually increase their wealth, but it also carries some risk.

Purchasing stock in a firm that is publicly traded is one form of investing in stocks. Depending on the company's success and the status of the stock market as a whole, the stock's value may increase or decrease. An investor may sell the shares for a profit when the value increases. The investor might lose money, however, if the stock's value declines.

Purchasing digital currencies like Bitcoin or Ethereum to invest in cryptocurrencies with the hope of making a profit is known as cryptocurrency investing. Cryptocurrency prices have the potential to change drastically and quickly. Investments in cryptocurrencies are regarded as high-risk and not appropriate for all investors.

Options, futures, and currency trading are other types of internet trading. Not all investors should participate in these kinds of investments since they include risks.

Before engaging in any kind of online trading, it is crucial to carry out in-depth research and comprehend the hazards involved. Additionally, it is essential to have a clear grasp of how the market functions and a solid risk management plan in place.

RESEARCH GUIDELINES FOR REDUCING RISK

A series of instructions or suggestions for people or organizations wanting to trade in stocks, cryptocurrencies, or other kinds of online trading is referred to as "tips for studying and limiting risk." These guidelines are intended to assist investors in doing in-depth research, comprehending the risks, and making educated choices that will reduce the likelihood of loss.

Here are some pointers for doing your homework and reducing risk while trading stocks, cryptocurrencies, or other securities online:

1. Understand the Market: Before making an investment, it's crucial to comprehend the fundamentals of the market's

operation and the dangers involved. This entails researching the various investment options, as well as their prospective rewards and hazards.

2. Diversify Your Portfolio: By investing in a variety of different assets, you may help spread risk and lessen the effect that any one investment will have on your portfolio as a whole.

3. Exercise Due Care: Do your homework on the business or cryptocurrency you are thinking about investing in, including a look at its management, finances, and track record. Keep an eye out for warning signs like significant debt or insider selling.

4 . Use stop-loss orders, which are orders sent to a broker to sell a security when it hits a certain price. In the event that the market swings against the deal, this might assist to minimise losses.

5. Keep An Eye On The News: Keep abreast of political and economic developments that may have an influence on the market, and be ready to change your investments as necessary.

6 . The value of assets may vary quickly, so it's crucial to be ready for volatility and have a strategy in place for managing risk. 6. Be Prepared For Volatility

7. Seek Professional Counsel: It could be a good idea to seek professional advice from a financial adviser or other trained professional if you are uncomfortable with the amount of risk or unsure of your capacity for research.

8 . Always invest with prudence and never put more money at risk than you can afford to lose. This brings us to number eight.

These suggestions are designed to be broad recommendations, but it's vital to keep in mind that each person's financial position is different and that previous success doesn't guarantee future performance.

CHAPTER 4:

RESEARCH STUDIES AND SURVEYS

Methods for acquiring data and information on a particular subject or group include surveys and research projects. Research studies are more thorough investigations that use a variety of methodologies to gather data and make inferences, as opposed to surveys, which are a tool for gathering information from a sample of people using a standardized questionnaire.

Participants often fill out online surveys on their own devices, such as laptops or cellphones, utilizing the internet to conduct them.

These questionnaires may be used for a variety of things, including market research, product creation, and academic study.

On the other hand, research studies are deeper examinations that use a range of techniques to gather information and make judgments.

These investigations might be experimental, observational, or clinical trials. They may be used for a variety of goals, including studying customer behavior, gauging the efficacy of novel goods or services, or discovering new information on a specific subject. They are often carried out by researchers, academics, or companies.

Participants might be compensated for their time and participation in surveys and research projects that are done online. However, it's crucial to be aware that not all survey and research firms are reliable, and some may gather personal information or demand payment in advance. As a result, it's crucial to conduct your homework and exercise caution.

Another approach to earning money online while at home is to take part in online surveys and research projects. To obtain information and insights on a variety of subjects, including customer behavior, market trends, and product development, businesses and organizations undertake research projects. People are often paid to do surveys, engage in focus groups, or test items as part of these studies.

Companies that conduct online surveys and research studies include:
JUNKIE
SWAGBUCKS
TOLUNA
SURVEY.
Online Harris Poll on American Consumer Opinion conducted by Vindale Research

CONSULTATION JUNKIE A website called Junkie links people with businesses and organizations asking for customer feedback. Users may join up for a free account and then participate in surveys on a variety of subjects, including politics, entertainment, and consumer goods. Users who complete surveys on the website are paid in the form of points, which can be exchanged for money or gift cards.

Through the Survey Junkie website or the Survey Junkie app, which is accessible for iOS and Android devices, users may access surveys. The surveys range in length and may be finished in as little as a few minutes or as long as

30. Each poll offers a different number of points, with lengthier surveys often awarding more.

With a solid reputation and a large number of pleased consumers, Survey Junkie is regarded as a reliable survey website. Users have given it a 4-star rating on Trustpilot and praised the range of surveys and simplicity of use. However, the earning potential is limited, and there may not always be enough surveys accessible, as on other survey websites.

SWAGBUCKS

Users of the website and mobile app Swagbucks get rewards for carrying out various online tasks including completing surveys, viewing videos, and online shopping. The website provides a large selection of surveys on a variety of subjects, such as consumer goods, entertainment, and politics. For every survey taken, users may accumulate "Swagbucks" points, which can be exchanged for money or gift cards.

Through the Swagbucks website or the mobile app, which is accessible on iOS and Android devices, users may access surveys. The surveys range in length and may be finished in as little as a few minutes or as long as 30. Each survey offers a different number of Swagbucks, with lengthier polls often offering more.

With a positive online presence and a large number of pleased users, Swagbucks is regarded as a reliable survey and incentive website. Users have given it a 4-star rating on Trustpilot and praised the range of activities and simplicity of use. However, the earning potential is limited, and there may not always be enough surveys accessible, as on other survey websites.

TOLUNA

Users who complete surveys and share their thoughts on a variety of subjects are rewarded by the online survey platform Toluna. Users may join up for a free account and then participate in surveys on a variety of subjects, including politics, entertainment, and consumer goods. Users who complete surveys on the website are paid in the form of points, which can be exchanged for money or gift cards.

The Toluna website and mobile app, which is accessible on iOS and Android devices, both allow users to access surveys. The surveys range in length and may be finished in as little as a few minutes or as long as 30. Each poll offers a different number of points, with lengthier surveys often awarding more.

Toluna is regarded as a trustworthy survey platform with a large user base of happy customers. Users have given it a 4-star rating on Trustpilot and praised the range of surveys and simplicity of use. However, the earning potential is limited, and there may not always be enough surveys accessible, as on other survey websites.

AMERICA CONSUMER OPINION

Users who complete surveys and share their ideas on different issues are rewarded by the survey panel American Consumer Opinion (ACOP). Users may join up for a free account and then participate in surveys on a variety of subjects, including politics, entertainment, and consumer goods. Users who complete surveys on the website are paid in cash, and payments may be done using PayPal or a cheque.

Surveys may be accessed via the American Consumer Opinion website, and users get email invites to participate. The surveys range in length and may be finished in as little as a few minutes or as long as 30. Each survey's earnings potential varies as well, with lengthier polls often yield higher payouts.

ACOP is regarded as a reliable survey panel with a solid reputation and plenty of happy consumers. It is a market research organization that has been conducting customer surveys since 1986. However, the earning potential is limited, and there may not always be enough surveys accessible, as on other survey websites.

THE HARRIS POLL

Users get prizes from the market research firm Harris Poll Online for completing surveys and contributing their thoughts on different subjects. Users may join up for a free account and then participate in surveys on a variety of subjects, including politics, entertainment, and consumer goods. Users who complete surveys on the website are paid in the form of points, which can be exchanged for money or gift cards.

Through the Harris Poll Online website or the Harris Poll app, which is accessible for iOS and Android devices, users may access surveys. The surveys range in length and may be finished in as little as a few minutes or as long as 30. Each poll offers a different number of points, with lengthier surveys often awarding more.

With a solid reputation and a large number of pleased consumers, Harris Poll Online is regarded as a reliable survey panel. One of the longest-running polls in the United States is The Harris Poll, and Harris Poll Online is the company's online division. It is a market research organization that has been conducting customer surveys since 1963. However, the earning potential is limited, and there may not always be enough surveys accessible, as on other survey websites.

THE VINDALE RESEARCH

Vindale Research is a market research firm that pays consumers for participating in surveys and giving feedback on different subjects. Users may join up for a free account and then participate in surveys on a variety of subjects, including politics, entertainment, and consumer goods. Users who complete surveys on the website are paid in cash, and payments may be done using PayPal or a cheque. On the Vindale Research website, users may access surveys, and email invites are also delivered. The surveys range in length and may be finished in as little as a few minutes or as long as 30. Each survey's earnings potential varies as well, with lengthier polls often yield higher payouts.

Vindale Research is regarded as a reliable survey panel with a solid reputation and a large number of happy consumers. It is a market research business that has been conducting customer surveys since 2005. They are renowned for paying more money than the majority of survey websites and for paying in cash rather than points. However, the earning potential is limited, and there may not always be enough surveys accessible, as on other survey websites.

The compensation for these surveys might vary and may not be particularly great, but taking part in online surveys and research projects can be a flexible and simple way to earn money from home.

Furthermore, it's crucial to be aware that not all survey and research businesses are reliable, and some may gather personal information or demand payment in advance. As a result, it's crucial to do careful research and exercise caution.

It's also crucial to keep in mind that certain research projects could demand that participants meet certain requirements, such as being a medical professional or having a certain degree of education.

TAKING PART IN ONLINE QUESTIONS OR ENROLLING IN PAID RESEARCH STUDIES

People may earn money online by offering their ideas and comments to businesses and organizations by taking part in online surveys or enrolling in paid research programs. Typically, online surveys include using a website or mobile app to respond to a series of questions on different subjects. Contrarily, paid research projects are in-depth analyses that could include taking part in focus groups, evaluating items, or filling out extensive questionnaires.

By registering with survey and research organizations like Survey Junkie, Swagbucks, Toluna, American Consumer Opinion, Harris Poll Online, and Vindale Research, anybody may take part in these studies. For completing surveys or taking part in research projects, these businesses generally provide cash or incentives like gift cards.

It's vital to keep in mind that earning potential from taking part in online surveys or research projects is limited, and the availability of surveys might vary. It's also crucial to conduct your homework and exercise caution since not all survey and research businesses are reliable.

IDENTIFYING LICENSED OPPORTUNITIES AND MAXIMIZING PROFITS

In the context of taking part in online surveys or enrolling in paid research studies, finding legitimate opportunities and maximizing earnings refers to the process of locating and taking advantage of reputable survey or research companies that offer fair compensation for the time and effort required to participate in their studies.

People may investigate survey and research firms online, reading reviews and looking for any red flags like requesting money beforehand or gathering personal information without authorization, in order to identify reputable possibilities. It's crucial to understand the earning potential, the number of accessible surveys, and the kinds of prizes provided, as well as the earning potential.

Utilizing as many valid survey or research opportunities as you can in order to earn the greatest money or prizes are referred to as "maximizing earnings." This might include registering with several survey or research firms, being picky about the surveys or studies you take part in, and being reliable with your survey or study completions. Additionally, being effective in your work and not wasting time is another way to maximize your earnings.

CHAPTER 5:

ONLINE TUTORING AND INSTRUCTION

The practice of instructing and supporting students in their academic endeavors remotely over the internet is referred to as online tutoring and teaching. This might include offering private tutoring, directing online seminars or courses, and producing and marketing instructional resources.

By giving students academic guidance and assistance remotely via the internet, online tutoring and teaching are methods to generate money online. Online instructors and tutors are available to help students of all ages and abilities, and they may focus on a range of areas, including math, science, language, and exam preparation.

For online tutoring and teaching, a number of platforms are available, including video conferencing software, virtual learning management systems, and pre-recorded video classes. Zoom, Skype, and Google Meet are a few of the well-liked systems that are often used for online education and tutoring.

Online instructors and tutors have two options: they may either work on their own, determining their hours and fees, or they can partner with an organization that matches them with students. Several well-known online teaching and tutoring businesses

include Chegg Tutors, TutorMe, and VIPKid.
VIPKID

An online education startup called VIPKid links English instructors with Chinese students for individualized

English language teaching. Teachers may work remotely and earn money online from their homes with VIPKid.

Candidates need a bachelor's degree and previous child-care experience to serve as VIPKid instructors. Additionally, they must pass a mock interview and finish a certification program. Once qualified, instructors are free to choose their own hours and do business from any location with a reliable internet connection.

The VIPKid platform is simple to use, and instructors provide lessons via an online classroom. Teachers may make between $14 and $22 per hour for each 25-minute lesson they offer. Additionally, VIPKid rewards instructors for maintaining high attendance rates and for recommending other educators to the site.

With a solid reputation and a large number of pleased instructors, VIPKid is regarded as a reliable online tutoring business. The earning potential is limited, as it is with any online tutoring business, and the availability of programs might fluctuate.

TUTOR

With the help of the online tutoring platform TutorMe, students may get individualized training from tutors in a range of areas.

Tutors may assist children of various ages and academic levels, and they can focus on a variety of areas, such as math, science, language, and test-taking strategies. Another option for tutoring is via pre-recorded video classes, live video sessions, or sessions based on chat.

Candidates must have a bachelor's degree and have teaching or subject-matter experience in order to tutor on TutorMe.

A background check, online application, and interview procedure are also required. Tutors who are hired may choose their own hours and fees, and they can work from any location with a reliable internet connection.

To connect and collaborate, instructors and students may utilize the user-friendly platform provided by TutorMe. Payments are done via the site, and tutors may make $15 to $30 per hour.

Additionally, TutorMe rewards instructors for suggesting other tutors to the site and for maintaining high student satisfaction ratings.

With a solid reputation and a large number of pleased instructors, TutorMe is regarded as a reliable online tuition provider.

The earning potential is limited, as it is with any online tutoring business, and the availability of programs might fluctuate.

CHEGG TEACHERS

Through its online tutoring platform, Chegg Tutors, students may get individualized instruction from tutors in a range of areas.

There are many other disciplines available on the site, such as math, science, English, social studies, and exam preparation. Another option for tutoring is via pre-recorded video classes, live video sessions, or sessions based on chat.

Candidates for Chegg Tutors must have a bachelor's degree and have experience in teaching or the subject topic being tutored.

A background check, online application, and interview procedure are also required. Tutors who are hired may choose their own hours and fees, and they can work from any location with a reliable internet connection.

The learning environment may be improved by teachers using technologies like a virtual whiteboard and file sharing on the user-friendly platform. Payments are done via the site, and tutors may make $20 to $30 per hour. Additionally, Chegg Instructors rewards tutors for suggesting other tutors to the site and for maintaining a high student satisfaction rating.

With a solid reputation and a large number of pleased instructors, Chegg Tutors is regarded as a reliable online tutoring service. The earning potential is limited, as it is with any online tutoring business, and the availability of programs might fluctuate.

For individuals with teaching or subject matter experience, as well as for those who feel at ease working in an online setting, online tutoring and teaching may be a flexible and gratifying way to earn money online from home.

BY USING APPLICATIONS LIKE VIPKID OR TEACHABLE, PROVIDING VIRTUAL TUTORING OR TEACHING

The practice of giving educational instruction and assistance to students remotely via the internet through the use of specialized online platforms, such as VIPKid or Teachable, is known as offering virtual tutoring or teaching.

Through these platforms, anyone may produce and sell their own online courses or provide private tutoring sessions. By imparting their knowledge and experience to students through these platforms, people may earn money online in a simple and adaptable manner. By selling courses, they also provide the possibility of passive income.

An online education startup called VIPKid links English instructors with Chinese students for individualized English language teaching. Candidates need a bachelor's degree and previous child-care experience to serve as VIPKid instructors.

On the Teachable platform, users may design and market their online courses. It offers resources including marketing, hosting, payment processing, and course design tools. Individuals must first register an account with Teachable before they can start designing and promoting their courses.

SUCCESSFUL ONLINE TEACHING BUSINESS GUIDELINES

There are several suggestions and tactics that people may use to launch and expand their online teaching businesses. These are tips for developing a successful online teaching company. With the aid of these suggestions, people may establish a powerful and successful presence in the online teaching market, draw in more students, and boost their earning potential.

1. Identify Your Niche: Concentrate on a certain topic or talent that you are knowledgeable about and enthusiastic about. This will make you stand out in a congested market and draw in a certain audience.

2. Create high-quality course materials, including videos, PDFs, and quizzes, by devoting time and effort to their

creation. Make your information engaging and student-friendly by incorporating multimedia into it.

3. Create a website or utilize an online learning platform to display your credentials, expertise, and recommendations. 3. Develop a Professional Profile. Make connections with prospective students and advertise your company via social media.

4. Reach out to other educators, become involved in online groups, and go to networking events to cultivate connections and market your company. To reach a larger audience, use paid advertising, email marketing, and content marketing.

5. Constantly Improve: Continue to study and develop as a teacher. Ask for input from your students, then incorporate it into your teaching strategies and course materials. Keep abreast with the most recent developments and ideal procedures in online education.

6. Set Reasonable Fees: Conduct market research to see what other instructors are charging for comparable services, and base your rates on that information. To draw in new pupils, be prepared to haggle and provide discounts.

7. Be responsive and organized, and be accessible to help students with their inquiries. Organize your timetable, and let students know if anything is going to alter.

Make sure you have a dependable internet connection, a top-notch microphone and camera, and a peaceful environment to teach. A professional setting will contribute to the pupils' having a better learning experience.

CHAPTER 6 :

ONLINE COURSES AND E-BOOKS

Digital educational resources that may be accessed and studied online are referred to as online courses and e-books. They may be produced and marketed by people, corporations, or educational organizations, and they can be used to teach a range of topics, skills, or information.

Online courses may contain videos, quizzes, and exams and are often interactive and self-paced. They may be made available via several channels, including individual websites or MOOCs (Massive Open Online Courses). Online courses sometimes come with certificates or accreditation and are typically more thorough than e-books.

On the other hand, e-books are electronic copies of books that can be read on computers, tablets, or e-readers. They may provide a more in-depth analysis of a subject than an online course and are often used for non-fiction themes.

You may create and sell e-books and online courses to those who are interested in mastering a certain topic to make money online. Additionally, they provide consumers with a flexible and convenient method to advance their education from the comfort of their own homes.

Making and promoting digital goods like e-books or online courses

Sharing one's knowledge and experience with others via the creation and sale of digital items like online courses and e-books is a method for people to earn money online. These goods may be produced and sold on a number of online marketplaces, including Udemy, Coursera, and personal websites.

It's crucial to choose a niche or subject that you are knowledgeable about and enthusiastic about while establishing a digital product. Your product will become more enticing to prospective buyers and help you draw in a more narrowly focused audience.

Success also requires producing top-notch, interesting material. Using multimedia to make the information interactive, offering worthwhile and educational content, and making sure the course or e-book is simple to browse are all examples of how to do this.

Once the digital product is finished, it's critical to advertising it successfully in order to appeal to a larger audience. Social media, paid advertising, email marketing, and content marketing may all be used for this.

Selling digital goods online may be a practical, adaptable method to earn money while also offering the possibility of passive revenue. A defined target audience and efficient marketing are crucial for the success of digital product creation and sales, which need significant time and effort commitment.

SUGGESTIONS FOR GENERATING HIGH-QUALITY CONTENT AND EFFECTIVE MARKETING

A series of suggestions and tactics may be used by people to make sure that their digital goods, such as online courses or e-books, are well-received by their target audience and efficiently marketed to reach a broader audience. These tips are for producing high-quality content and marketing effectively.

Producing Excellent Content

1. Determine Who Your Demographic Is and What They Want From A Digital Product by identifying your target audience.
2. Select a focused area of study or a niche: Develop your skills in a field in which you have a keen interest.
3. Make Use of Multimedia: Include music, video, and graphics in your material to make it more interactive and interesting for students.
4. Provide value by making sure that your information is educational, practical, and applicable.
5. Maintain organization: To make it simple to explore, use headings and subheadings with a uniform layout.

MARKETING SUCCESSFULLY:

1. Create A Website Or Use An Online Platform: To promote your services and credentials, build a website or use an online learning platform.
2. Use social media: Connect with prospective clients and advertise your company via social media.
3. Reach out to other educators, become involved in online groups, and go to networking events to foster connections and market your company.
4. Make use of paid advertising, email marketing, and content marketing to expand your audience and boost exposure.
5. Constantly Improve: Continue to study and develop as a teacher. Ask for input from your students, then incorporate it into your teaching strategies and course materials.

Use SEO to your advantage by making your website, page titles, and meta descriptions search engine friendly.

Use influencer marketing to connect with your audience by collaborating with influencers in your field.

These guidelines may help people produce high-quality digital goods and sell them successfully to reach a larger audience, boost exposure, and enhance money.

CHAPTER 7:

SHORT-TERM RENTALS,

The practice of renting out a property, such as a home, apartment, or room, for a brief period of time, usually less than 30 days, is known as short-term rentals. This kind of rental is often arranged via internet marketplaces like Airbnb, VRBO, and Homeaway as an alternative to conventional long-term rentals or hotels. Renting out their house to visitors, tourists, or business travelers may be a method for homeowners to earn additional money.

AIRBNB

Through the web marketplace Airbnb, people may offer short-term rentals of their houses or flats to tourists. Having been established in 2008, it is now one of the most well-known short-term rental platforms in the world, with millions of listings spread throughout more than 100,000 locations.

Airbnb enables homeowners to rent out their residences to visitors, whether they are on holiday or on business, who can browse and reserve accommodations online. It offers a handy alternative for property owners to generate additional money from their investments and for tourists to locate unusual and economical lodging choices.

Private rooms in a shared area are one of the many property categories that Airbnb provides, in addition to whole houses and flats. A wide range of amenities is also provided, including Wi-Fi, a kitchen, and laundry facilities.

The platform manages payments and gives both hosts and visitors insurance. Additionally, it provides a ranking system and reviews so that hosts and guests may assess one another. This helps to increase trust and confidence in the platform.

While renting out your house on Airbnb may be a terrific way to earn money online from home, there are hazards and obligations involved. Before marketing your home, it's crucial to do some research on the local ordinances and rules as well as insurance coverage.

VRBO

Through the internet rental marketplace VRBO, people may offer short-term rentals of their houses, flats, or vacation properties to tourists. Since its founding in 1995, it has grown to become one of the most well-known short-term rental platforms in the world, with more than 2 million listings spread over 190 countries.

Similar to Airbnb, VRBO enables house owners to rent out their spaces to visitors, whether they are on holiday or on business, who can browse and book accommodations online. It provides a variety of property types, including whole houses, apartments, and villas as well as single rooms and cabins.

Depending on the property, the platform also provides a range of extras including Wi-Fi, kitchen and laundry facilities, private pools, and hot tubs. In addition to offering hosts and visitors insurance coverage, VRBO offers a secure payment method.

Additionally, it provides a ranking system and reviews so that hosts and guests may assess one another. This helps to increase trust and confidence in the platform. Although renting out a house via VRBO is a terrific method for homeowners to earn money online from home, there are hazards and obligations involved. Before marketing your home, it's crucial to do some research on the local ordinances and rules as well as insurance coverage.

HOMEAWAY
Through the internet rental marketplace HomeAway, people may offer short-term rentals of their houses, flats, or vacation homes to tourists. With more than 2 million listings in 190 countries, it was established in 2005 and is now among the most well-known short-term rental platforms worldwide.

Similar to Airbnb and VRBO, HomeAway enables homeowners to rent out their houses to vacationers, business travelers, and other people looking for lodging online. It provides a variety of property types, including whole houses, apartments, and villas as well as single rooms and cabins.

Depending on the property, the platform also provides a range of extras including Wi-Fi, kitchen and laundry facilities, private pools, and hot tubs. In addition to offering hosts and visitors insurance, HomeAway offers a safe payment method.

Additionally, it provides a ranking system and reviews so that hosts and guests may assess one another. This helps to increase trust and confidence in the platform. HomeAway is a fantastic method for property owners to earn money online by renting out their houses, but it also has certain dangers and obligations. Before marketing your home, it's crucial to do some research on the local ordinances and rules as well as insurance coverage.

Since they involve little capital and provide you the opportunity to generate money while you're gone, short-term rentals might be a terrific method to earn money online from home. The management of cleaning and upkeep, dealing with visitors, and adhering to local laws are some of the problems that come with it. Before marketing your home, it's crucial to do some research on the local ordinances and rules as well as insurance coverage.

Additionally, it's important to be ready for the duties that come with being a landlord, including upkeep and resolving crises. Although it's not for everyone, short-term renting may be a terrific option to earn money online from home. Before getting started, it's crucial to examine the benefits and drawbacks and determine if it fits your objectives and lifestyle.

RENT YOUR CAR ON TURO OR A SPARE ROOM ON AIRBNB

You may generate money online by renting out assets you already possess by listing a spare room on Airbnb or your automobile on Turo.

While Turo enables people to hire out their own vehicles to others, Airbnb enables people to rent out a spare room in their house to tourists. Both platforms are intended to make it simple for users to profit from assets they already possess but don't use often.

By renting out a property that isn't being utilized by tourists, renting out a spare room on Airbnb may be a terrific way to generate some additional money. However, it also entails certain duties, like upkeep, provision of necessities, and interaction with visitors.

You may make money by renting out a vehicle that you don't use all the time by renting it out on Turo. In addition to providing you with the opportunity to choose your own automobile rental rates and timetable, Turo also handles payments for you.

Before putting your house or automobile on the market, it's crucial to understand the applicable local ordinances and insurance requirements. You should also be aware of your obligations as a landlord or car owner and be ready for them.

How to Maximize Profits and Deliver Outstanding Customer Service

When renting out a spare room or a vehicle on Airbnb or Turo, here are some tips to help you maximize your earnings and provide top-notch customer service:

1. Set a competitive price for your room or automobile by comparing it to those for nearby listings that are comparable to yours.

2. Use high-quality photographs and a thorough description to make your ad stand out and attract more prospective tenants or visitors.

3. Be prompt in your responses to questions and communications to improve your chances of getting a reservation.

4. Be open and honest about any regulations or limitations, such as no smoking and no pets, to prevent misunderstandings or disappointments.
5. Deliver excellent customer service: Be approachable, and helpful, and give tenants and visitors all the information they need to have a wonderful stay or vacation.
6. Be flexible with check-in and check-out times: Be accommodating of your visitors' or tenants' schedules by being flexible with check-in and check-out timings.
7. Maintain your vehicle or property: Keep your vehicle or property clean, maintained, and in excellent functioning order.
8. Encourage favorable feedback from visitors or tenants to assist draw in more business in the future.
Use smart locks, cameras, and keyless access to simplify check-in and check-out for visitors or tenants.
9. Use technology to automate operations.
Maintain open lines of contact with visitors or tenants during their stay or vacation to make sure they have a wonderful time and to handle any problems that may come up.
These pointers can help you grow revenue and provide excellent customer service, which will boost bookings and enhance your reputation.

CHAPTER 8 :

ASSISTANCE VIRTUAL

The term "virtual help" describes the distant, usually online, delivery of administrative, technical, or creative services to customers. A virtual assistant (VA) works for themselves and offers customers expert support from a home office or another distant location.

A broad variety of activities, including email response, appointment setting, social media management, data input, research, customer support, event planning, and more, may be included in virtual help.

Virtual assistants often have specialized knowledge or expertise in a certain field and may work with one or many customers. Having a flexible schedule and the ability to work from any location at any time makes virtual assistants a common option for professionals, entrepreneurs, and small business owners.

The development of the internet and the emergence of entrepreneurs and small company owners who want help with a variety of jobs but do not want to engage a full-time employee have both contributed to the growth of the virtual assistance sector in recent years.

The ability to utilize one's knowledge and expertise to assist companies and entrepreneurs while simultaneously having the freedom to work from any location and establish one's own hours makes virtual assistance a terrific method to earn money online from home.

WEBSITES LIKE ZIRTUAL, PROVIDING VIRTUAL ASSISTANCE SERVICES

People may earn money online by delivering administrative, technical, or creative skills to customers remotely by offering virtual support services on websites like Zirtual.

Zirtual is a platform that links companies and company owners with virtual assistants (VAs) that can assist with a variety of duties including organizing appointments, handling emails, doing research, writing content, and more. The platform enables customers to identify, employ, and collaborate with virtual assistants on a flexible basis, either on an ongoing basis or for specific projects.

You may choose your own fees, establish your own hours, and work with customers from all around the globe as a virtual assistant on Zirtual. You must possess the necessary knowledge and expertise for the jobs you wish to provide, as well as a computer and internet connection, in order to be qualified to work on Zirtual.

You should be aware that being a virtual assistant on Zirtual or any other platform may include meeting specific criteria and regulations, including passing a background check. You may also be asked to sign a contract with the business.

Although you may utilize your knowledge and expertise to assist companies and entrepreneurs, working as a virtual assistant on Zirtual can be a terrific way to earn money online from home since you have the freedom to work from anywhere and on your own time.

SUCCESSFUL VIRTUAL ASSISTANCE BUSINESS GUIDELINES

A series of rules or suggestions that might aid those who wish to launch a virtual assistance company in setting up, expanding, and maintaining their firm is known as tips for developing a successful virtual assistance business.

Guidelines for creating a profitable virtual support business:

1. Identify your Niche: To make it simpler to get customers, focus on a certain area of expertise, such as social media management, email marketing, or data entry.
2. Create a professional portfolio of your work to demonstrate your abilities and expertise.
3. Network: Engage in online discussions with other virtual assistants, participate in online groups and forums, and attend virtual events to meet prospective employers.
4. Build a professional website to display your services, a portfolio of your work, and your contact details.
5. Create a clear service offering by outlining your offerings in order to attract customers and establish expectations.
6. Communicate Effectively: To gain a client's trust and create a productive working relationship, be quick to respond, approachable, and professional.
7. Maintain Organization: To remain on top of your workload and fulfill deadlines, use tools like calendars, task lists, and project management software.
8. In order to continually enhance your services, keep abreast of market developments, cutting-edge technology, and best practices.

9. Encourage customers to submit favorable reviews, which will help draw in new customers.
10. Be Open To Input: To better understand your customer's demands and provide better services, be open to feedback from them.

You may create a profitable virtual help company and gradually expand your clientele by using the advice in this article. Even though it takes time and effort, you can create a company that gives you a reliable income and the freedom to work from anywhere if you have a solid plan and a strong work ethic.

CHAPTER 9:

DROPSHIPPING

Dropshipping is a business strategy where a corporation sells things without keeping them on hand. Instead, the corporation buys the item from a third-party supplier and sends it straight to the consumer once a customer placed an order.

This enables the business to provide a variety of items without having to manage shipping and logistics or have a physical inventory.

Because it often entails minimal initial costs and ease of scalability, dropshipping is a well-known e-commerce business strategy.

The company owner simply has to worry about marketing and sales since the supplier takes care of all inventory management, packing, and shipping.

This enables a lean company strategy and a more adaptable way of living.

SHOPIFY, ALIEXPRESS, and OBERLO are a few of the well-liked dropshipping platforms.

SHOPIFY

An online shop may be created and managed by both individuals and companies using the Shopify e-commerce platform. It offers several tools and services, including a website builder, payment processing, inventory management, shipping, and tax tools, to assist customers in setting up and running their online businesses. The simplicity with which Shopify can interact with various plugins and applications, including those that facilitate dropshipping, is one of its most well-liked features.

Shopify also provides a selection of editable templates and design alternatives that make it simple for users to construct a website that looks professional. It also provides a selection of SEO and marketing tools to assist users in promoting their stores and boosting exposure online. Additionally, Shopify has an integrated blog tool that enables shop owners to add content to their website and raise their website's search engine exposure.

Small business owners and entrepreneurs often choose to dropship using Shopify because it is simple to set up and maintain an online shop and because it provides a variety of tools and integrations that assist dropshipping. It is also a trustworthy platform with a solid reputation, which makes it a preferred option for company owners.

ALIEXPRESS

An online marketplace called Aliexpress is run by the Chinese-based Alibaba Group. Although it resembles other online marketplaces like Amazon and eBay, its main emphasis is on small enterprises and independent sellers from China and other nations. A variety of things are available on Aliexpress, including fashion, household goods, electronics, and more.

AliExpress is often used for dropshipping. Aliexpress is a popular resource for dropshippers to locate goods to offer in their online shops. Dropshippers just choose an item on AliExpress that they wish to sell, decide on a price, and then upload the item to their own shop. The drop shipper puts the order on Aliexpress on behalf of the client and arranges for the supplier to send the goods straight to the customer. Because of this, the drop shipper may sell a variety of goods without having to manage their own shipping and logistics or have a physical inventory.

For dropshippers, Aliexpress has a lot to offer, including a large selection of items, affordable rates, and quick delivery choices. To enhance the security of transactions, it also provides a secure payment mechanism and a buyer protection program. Dropshipping from Aliexpress may have some potential drawbacks, however, including the possibility of issues with quality control and lengthier shipping delays than other choices.

OBERLO

Oberlo is a Shopify software that enables customers to quickly import and sell goods from the well-known Chinese online retailer AliExpress. Users can quickly select items to sell, add them to their Shopify shop, and complete purchases with just a few clicks thanks to this tool. Oberlo is a practical option for people wishing to launch a dropshipping company since it also automatically manages inventory and adjusts prices.

Oberlo's ability to import goods straight from AliExpress, which has a huge selection of goods at low rates, is one of its important benefits. Before adding the imported goods to their shop, Oberlo users may further modify them by altering the product names, descriptions, and photos.

Additionally, Oberlo has an integrated order fulfillment system that enables users to make orders with suppliers and check the progress of such orders. Furthermore, it enables customers to swiftly complete several purchases with only a few clicks, which may save a great deal of time and work.

Overall, drop shippers choose Oberlo because it makes it simple to launch a company and automates many of the duties involved in managing an online shop. For individuals who wish to launch a company with little initial expenses and little inventory maintenance, it is a perfect option.

STARTING A DROPSHIPPING COMPANY AND FORMING A PARTNERSHIP WITH A SUPPLIER

Create an online shop, locate a supplier, and then list the goods you want to sell on your site to start a dropshipping company. You will buy the item when a client puts in an order, and your supplier will send it to the customer on your behalf.

A crucial step in starting a dropshipping company is forming a partnership with a supplier. A supplier is a business or person that supplies the goods you'll offer on your internet shop. The manufacture, storage, and delivery of the goods to your clients are within the purview of the supplier. To make sure that your consumers are happy, it's crucial to take into account elements like product quality, pricing, and delivery timeframes when picking a supplier.

A reputable provider will offer a variety of goods at reasonable rates with quick delivery alternatives.

Additionally, it's critical to check that your provider offers excellent customer service, is trustworthy, and is simple to get a hold of.

In conclusion, starting a dropshipping company entails setting up an internet shop, locating a supplier, and then adding the items you want to sell to your site. Finding a supplier that can satisfy your company objectives and provide high-quality items to your clients involves the study and due diligence. Partnering with a supplier is an essential stage in the process.

SUGGESTIONS FOR IDENTIFYING THE RIGHT GOODS AND SUPPLIERS AND GETTING RID OF POSSIBLE PROBLEMS .

A collection of rules and techniques may assist a company owner in identifying successful items, and dependable suppliers, and minimizing risks connected with drop shipping operations. These tips can also help them overcome possible problems.

There are a few important considerations to bear in mind while locating items and suppliers for a dropshipping business:

1. Before beginning your dropshipping company, it's crucial to do market research and choose a certain niche or product category that you want to concentrate on. This will enable you to focus your product search and identify

vendors who are experts in the market area you have selected.

2. Search for high-demand products: It's crucial to choose goods with a high level of demand when choosing what to offer. By doing this, you may increase the likelihood that your shop will be profitable.

3. Locate trustworthy suppliers: It's critical to choose trustworthy suppliers that can be relied upon to offer high-quality goods and attentive customer care. This entails seeking vendors that have a solid reputation, have competitive pricing, and provide quick shipment.

4. Test your items to make sure they satisfy your requirements for quality before putting them on your store's shelves. Ordering a sample or reading customer feedback are two ways to do this.

5. Recognize the legal requirements: It's essential to be aware of and compliant with the legal standards that apply to dropshipping. For instance, you must inform your clients that you drop ship and that you could charge taxes.

It might be challenging to overcome potential obstacles, but there are a few ways to reduce the risk:

1. Maintain a diverse product range to reduce the possibility of having most of your sales come from just one or two items.

2. Keep in touch with your suppliers: A successful business relationship depends on good communication with your suppliers.

3. Maintain an eye on your inventory: Keep track of your stock to make sure you don't run out of items and can quickly satisfy requests.

4. Constantly tweak your marketing tactics: To keep your shop visible and draw in more consumers, constantly tweak your marketing tactics.

5. Remain informed: To assist you to stay one step ahead of the competition, keep up with the most recent e-commerce industry developments, legislation, and best practices.

CONCLUSION :

In conclusion, there are several options to work from home and earn money online in 2023.

Creating an online business and working with a supplier to sell goods without keeping a physical inventory is known as drop shipping.

Offering services such as writing, graphic design, or programming via websites like Upwork or Fiverr is known as freelancing.

Participating in internet surveys or enrolling in for-profit research projects

Stock and cryptocurrency investing: Investing in stocks, cryptocurrencies, or other online trading methods

Online tutoring and teaching: Using services like VIPKid or Teachable to provide virtual tuition or instruction

online shopping, Online shops, and markets using websites like Etsy or Amazon to reach a larger audience

Building a following on blogs and YouTube while making money via advertising, affiliate marketing, or sponsored content

By using websites like Zirtual, you may provide virtual help services.

Renting out a spare room on Airbnb or your automobile on Turo are examples of short-term rentals.

E-books and Online Courses: Producing and promoting digital goods like e-books and online courses.
encouragement to act and launch a new internet business.

In 2023 and beyond, starting an internet business might be a terrific way to earn money from home. Anyone can launch a profitable internet company with the appropriate strategy and some effort. Find a company model that works for you, identify your talents and services, and conduct your study. There are several methods to earn money online from home, including dropshipping, freelancing, online surveys, trading stocks or cryptocurrencies, online teaching, and online tutoring.

It's crucial to keep in mind that launching an internet business needs perseverance, patience, and hard work. There will be obstacles in your path, but don't let them deter you; they are a necessary component of every firm. It's crucial to keep growing and learning since this will help you succeed over time.

Therefore, start your investigation into the many methods to generate money online right now if you're seeking a new approach to working from home in 2023. You may make your internet company effective and lucrative with the appropriate attitude and work.

This is a broad summary of the several options to work from home and earn money online in 2023. One has to do a more thorough investigation and compile more data and examples to have comprehensive guidance on any of the things listed. It's also vital to consider any certificates or credentials that could be necessary to follow certain career pathways, as well as the various rules, regulations, and taxes that may be necessary for each sort of internet company. It's crucial to think about any dangers and difficulties associated with each alternative, as well as to consult experts when necessary.

www.ingramcontent.com/pod-product-compliance
Lightning Source LLC
Chambersburg PA
CBHW070320220526
45465CB00013B/1794